Would you rather hold hands or hug?

Would you rather kiss me on my cheek or kiss me on my forehead?

Would you rather be funny or good-looking?

Would you rather give up sex or the internet for the rest of your life?

Would you rather get a kiss on the cheeks after the first date or get a kiss on the lips after the first date?

Would you rather die a virgin or be a horrible person for your entire life?

Would you rather be poor and famous or rich with no friends?

Would you rather stay indoors and chill with your lover or go out with friends?

Would you rather have the perfect job or the perfect relationship?

Would you rather date an introvert or an extrovert?

Would you rather save a stranger's life or your beloved pet's life?

Would you rather have sex with someone you hate or never have sex?

Would you rather show a bit of skin when sending a selfie to your crush or show a lot of skin?

Would you rather Have it with the lights on or off?

Would you rather die a virgin or have a bunch of STDs?

Would you rather let your spouse date your best friend or your arch enemy?

Would you rather marry a rich girl or the girl you love?

Would you rather get hugs from the back or get hugs from the front?

Would you rather make out on a couch or make out against the wall?

Would you rather say something sweet to your partner or say something sexy to your partner?

Would you rather Have one partner or multiple partners?

Would you rather Talk with me about someone you fancy or fantasize about it secretly in your mind?

Would you rather Watch a girl on girl or guy on guy video, to turn yourself on?

Would you rather Watch something erotic with me, or read an erotica loud, while touching me?

Would you rather run your fingers through your partner's hair when kissing or across your partner's face?

Would you rather wear something hot to a night party with your partner or wear something hot on a dinner date with your partner?

Would you rather get compliments from a lot of people at a club or get compliments from just your crush?

Would you rather go out to watch a romantic movie with your crush or stay indoors to watch a romantic movie with your crush?

Would you rather try to make your partner jealous of someone or make everyone else jealous of your partner?

Would you rather give a sexy massage or get a sexy massage?

Would you rather kiss your partner in front of their parents or kiss your partner in front of their friends?

Would you rather cuddle under a blanket or cuddle beside a fireplace?

Would you rather tell your crush they have an amazing body or have your crush tell you that you have an amazing body?

Would you rather get a naughty nickname from your partner or give a naughty nickname to your partner?

Would you rather flirt with your crush using emojis while texting or using memes while texting?

Would you rather exchange a quick kiss with a co-worker or with your boss?

Would you rather be an exhibitionist or a shy person?

Would you rather give a hickey or be given a hickey?

Would you rather do porn or be poor?

Would you rather have a hot body and unattractive face or attractive face but and unattractive body?

Would you rather look amazing naked but only decent in clothes, or amazing in clothes but not great naked?

Would you rather have sex in a car or on an uncomfortable bed?

Would you rather die for your lover or have a lover who's willing to die for you?

Would you rather get the silence treatment or hurl words at each other when upset?

Would you rather be with a soldier or be with a terrorist?

Would you rather commit a crime with your lover or turn your lover in for a crime they committed?

Would you rather get a terrible gift for your birthday or no gift at all?

Would you rather your partner dumped you or you dumped your partner?

Would you rather wet the bed the first time your girlfriend spends the night or poop yourself doing squats in a public gym?

Would you rather be with someone really skinny or someone really huge?

Would you rather cuddle for five minutes or cuddle for five hours?

Would you rather hold my hand while you're driving or put your hand on my thigh?

Would you rather dance together under the sun or under the rain?

Would you rather be with someone who snores loudly or who talks in their sleep?

Would you rather have pillow fights together or food fights?

Would you rather kiss your partner after they ate a full garlic or after they told you they hadn't brushed in a week?

Would you rather steal your partner's shirt or steal your partner's shorts?

Would you rather date a comedian or date a clown?

Would you rather lick your partner all over or kiss your partner all over?

Would you rather be with someone who eats a lot or someone who plays with their food?

Would you rather try on your partner's clothes or have your partner try on your clothes?

Would you rather be with someone who smells funny or someone who likes to smell you?

Would you rather wear your partner's underwear or wear your dirty underwear?

Would you rather have a partner who never shaves or a partner who never uses deodorant?

Would you rather have quadruplets with your partner or have twins?

Would you rather your partner was a millionaire but a moron or was really broke but a genius?

Would you rather have a partner who sings in the shower or who sings while on the toilet seat?

Would you rather be with someone who laughs really loudly or someone who laughs really weirdly?

Would you rather have a partner with horrible dancing skills or one who's too hyper when they dance?

Would you rather draw a mustache over your partner's face when they're asleep or rub lipstick all over their mouth when they're asleep?

Would you rather tickle your partner till they start to laugh hysterically or tickle them till they start to cry?

Would you rather be with someone with zero fashion sense or someone with an outdated fashion sense?

Would you rather give a lap dance in public or get a lap dance in public?

Would you rather date a good kisser or date a good lover?

Would you rather stare into your partner's eyes or stare at your partner's lips?

Would you rather hold my hand while you're driving or put your hand on my thigh?

Would you rather give a strip tease or get a strip tease?

Would you rather cuddle up with your partner all night or make out with your partner all night?

Would you rather be purely physical with someone you like or make a serious commitment to someone you like?

Would you rather hold hands with your partner or wrap your arms around your partner?

Would you rather write a love letter or get a love letter?

Would you rather hit on someone you like via texting or hit on someone you like face-to-face?

Would you rather hit on someone much older than you or have someone much older hit on you?

Would you rather grind your partner on the dance floor or grind your partner in private?

Would you rather compliment your partner's physical features or have your partner compliment your physical features?

Would you rather kiss your partner's neck when making out or get neck kisses from your partner?

Would you rather run your hands all over your partner's body with the lights on or with the lights off?

Would you rather exchange a kiss under the stars or while watching the sunset?

Would you rather rub lotion on your partner's upper body or on your partner's lower body?

Would you rather make your partner moan or make your partner laugh?

Would you rather plan a surprise road trip with your partner or plan a surprise vacation with your partner?

Would you rather wear your partner's shirt or your partner's shorts?

Would you rather see a cute note from your partner in the morning or get a cute text from your partner in the afternoon?

Would you rather read a romantic novel together or watch a romantic movie together?

Would you rather turn your partner on with your lips or turn your partner on with your tongue??

Would you rather do a nude photo shoot with your partner or do a nude photo shoot with your partner watching?

Would you rather send a very revealing picture to your crush or get a very revealing picture from your crush?

Would you rather send your partner to a spa or give your partner a really good body treatment at home?

Would you rather buy a really sweet card for your crush or make a really sweet card for your crush?

Would you rather make out in an office chair or make out on an office table?

Would you rather write a poem expressing love felt for your crush or read a poem expressing love felt for you?

Would you rather dance under the moon or dance in pitch darkness?

Would you rather tell your partner about your sexual fantasies or have your partner tell you about their sexual fantasies??

Would you rather kiss your partner's chin or kiss your partner's nose?

Would you rather take a shower with your partner or climb into a bath with your partner?

Would you rather throw water balloons at your crush or spray water with a hose at your crush?

Would you rather watch your partner swim in a sexy bathing suit or have your partner watch you swim in a sexy bathing suit?

Would you rather buy a drink for a stranger you find attractive or have a stranger that finds you attractive buy you a drink?

Would you rather start your first date with sex or a romantic night out?

Would you rather cheat on your partner or get fired from your job?

Would you rather lick your soulmate or get licked by him/her?

Would you rather have a terrible relationship with great sex or have a great relationship with awful sex?

Would you rather receive an oral sex or give it?

Would you rather give up all fast food or give up oral sex?

Would you rather have no kids or three kids with disabilities?

Would you rather be caught cheating or have your soulmate cheat on you?

Would you rather never be able to have sex or never be able to eat your favorite food again?

Would you rather have an adorable kid with an embarrassing name or an awful kid with an adorable name?

Would you rather break someone's heart or have your heart broken by someone?

Would you rather intimate relationship with one partner or many partners?

Would you rather have sex with your soul mate or go on a romantic dinner?

Would you rather have everyone know about your sex life or your personal finances?

Would you rather get married to someone who is incredibly attractive or get attractive yourself?

Would you rather your partner was one who turned everything into a competition or one who was a sore loser?

Would you rather find a soul mate and have all your friends hate him or find a soul mate that hates all your friends?

Would you rather let your partner go through your WhatsApp texts or go through your Facebook messenger texts?

Would you rather have a partner who never has your time or a partner who's quite clingy?

Would you rather get married and never have kids or have kids and never get married?

Would you rather your partner loved your friends and hated your family or loved your family and hated your friends?

Would you rather be with someone who's very proud or someone with low self-esteem?

Would you rather serve burnt food for you both to eat or half-cooked food for you both to eat?

Would you rather watch a horror movie together or watch a tragedy movie together?

Would you rather tease your significant other with suggestive words or tease your significant other with suggestive actions?

Would you rather talk dirty to arouse your partner or have your partner talk dirty to arouse you?

Would you rather compliment your partner's butt in public or compliment your partner's butt in private?

Would you rather brush your lips across your crush's and make it look like an accident or kiss your crush?

Would you rather get a flattering statement from your ex or get a flattering statement from a stranger?

Would you rather catch your next door neighbor staring at you all the time or catch your landlord staring at you all the time?

Would you rather be known as someone who dresses to kill or be known as a smooth talker?

Would you rather throw yourself at a stranger who says all the right words or a stranger who touches you in all the right places?

Would you rather be cuddled by someone you like or be fondled by someone you like?

Would you rather go to your partner's place after the first date or invite your partner home after the first date?

Would you rather have a fling with your high school crush or with your celebrity crush?

Would you rather hit on a married person or be married and have someone hit on you?

Would you rather suggest a one night stand to your crush or suggest a one night stand to a stranger?

Would you rather blow a kiss at your crush from across the room or wink at your crush from across the room?

Would you rather whisper sweet words into your partner's ears or have your partner whisper sweet words into your ear?

Would you rather lean in to kiss your partner every time or have your partner lean in to kiss you every time?

Would you rather get on top of your partner's lap while they're seated or get on top of your partner while they're lying down?

Would you rather have pillow fights on the bed or wrestle one another on the bed?

Would you rather make out with your crush in a bathroom or in a closet?

Would you rather sing your heart out to your partner in private or in public?

Would you rather wake up to breakfast in bed or have your partner wake up to breakfast in bed?

Would you rather shower your partner with gifts or shower your partner with money?

Would you rather say "I love you" to your partner or show your partner just how much you love them?

Would you rather make out in a hotel's pool or in a hotel room's balcony?

Would you rather sext all day with your partner or sext all night with your partner?

Would you rather pin your partner down and cover them with kisses or have your partner pin you down and cover you with kisses?

Would you rather be handcuffed to the bed by your lover or handcuff your lover to the bed?

Would you rather grind each other on the dance floor or slow dance on the dance floor?

Would you rather have a snowball fight together or roll around in the snow together?

Would you rather give your partner a back rub or give your partner a foot rub?

Would you rather go to a bar with someone you like or go to a bar to meet someone new?

Would you rather have a random ex still flirting with you or flirt with your favorite ex?

Would you rather be the most sought after or have the most sought-after person as a partner?

Would you rather watch a stranger dance seductively or watch someone you know dance seductively?

Would you rather take a long walk side by side with your partner or go on a long drive side by side?

Would you rather go to a photo booth at a party together or take silly selfies at home together?

Would you rather light candles all over the bedroom or scatter roses all over the bed?

Would you rather play a romantic song on a piano for your partner or play a romantic song on a guitar?

Would you rather stick your hands under your partner's shirt or have your partner stick their hands under your shirt?

Would you rather chase your crush around at the beach or chase your crush around at a park?

Would you rather draw pictures in the sand with your partner or write your initials in the sand with your partner?

Would you rather Pay for having sex, or get paid for it?

Would you rather Swallow or spit?

Would you rather Be on top or underneath?

Would you rather Have sex with someone or watch someone having it?

Would you rather Have sex in the morning or at night?

Would you rather Receive an oral or give one?

Would you rather do romantic things or try out some new kinky ideas?

Would you rather be a famous singer or never known for who you are?

Would you rather marry someone who loves a political figure you hate or someone with a religious belief you hate?

Would you rather have a weird fetish or not have any fun?

Would you rather walk around naked in public or poop your pants in public?

Would you rather see your partner only on the weekdays but at work or only on the weekends at home?

Would you rather still be in contact with your ex or find out your significant other was still in contact with their ex?

Would you rather lose all your selfies or lose all your pictures with your significant other?

Would you rather your partner drove a rickety car or your partner didn't have a car at all?

Would you rather be with someone that talks a lot or someone who likes to keep things bottled up inside?

Would you rather your partner's mother didn't like you or your partner's father didn't like you?

Would you rather have a partner who thinks a lot or a partner who could never think for their self?

Would you rather have a partner who's antisocial or a partner who likes to be friends with everyone?

Would you rather have a partner who gets jealous all the time or a partner who makes you jealous all the time?

Would you rather be with someone who's a vegetarian or someone who's trying to get you to be a vegetarian?

Would you rather watch your partner dance with someone else or dance with your partner, even though you suck at it?

Would you rather meet your partner's parents first or have your partner meet your parents first?

Would you rather you both worked in the same office but earn peanuts or work in different countries and earn seven digit salaries?

Would you rather your partner had a lot of friends of the opposite gender or they had no friends at all?

Would you rather be with someone who has to go to bed late every night or one who has to get up early every morning?

Would you rather your partner was a celebrity with a lot of money but fans of the opposite sex, or your partner was unsuccessful and broke?

Would you rather live in a slum with your significant other or move into a decent place alone?

Would you rather abandon your partner to suffer the consequences of their sins or suffer with your partner?

Would you rather your partner worked for an ex they broke up with or worked for someone who hurt them the past?

Would you rather have a partner who was always stressed at work or a partner who constantly brings home all the stress of the day to pour it out on you?

Would you rather be with someone who's always on their phone or someone who's always going through your phone?

Would you rather date someone who likes to stay alone a lot or someone who enjoys the company of people a lot?

Would you rather be failures together or go your separate ways and become very successful?

Would you rather lie to them to protect their feelings or tell them the truth and hurt their feelings?

Would you rather share some bad news with your partner or have them find out at a later date on their own?

Would you rather have a partner who messes up the toilet occasionally or one who flares up at the slightest mess they notice in the toilet?

Would you rather your partner was broke and didn't tell anyone or your partner was broke and told only a close friend of the opposite sex?

Would you rather your partner broke an arm or broke a leg?

Would you rather your partner had a terrible addiction they couldn't drop or your partner had a terrible addiction that they refused to believe was bad?

Would you rather have a significant other who was too romantic and sweet or one who didn't know how to be romantic and sweet?

Would you rather your partner was an extremely rich person doing a shady business or a wretched person in a legal profession?

Would you rather wear your significant other's underwear or go out with no underwear?

Would you rather your significant other looked like a child or acted like a child?

Would you rather have a partner who eats really fast in public or one who chews really noisily in public?

Would you rather your partner had a much bigger head or a much smaller head?

Would you rather your partner had a house that looked bad or a house that smelt bad?

Would you rather your partner was the richest garbage man in the world or the poorest banker in the world?

Would you rather have a partner with a really squeaky voice or one with a crooked voice?

Would you rather be with someone who's very lazy and dirty or someone who's a clean freak?

Would you rather your partner was always overdressed to places or was always underdressed?

Would you rather have a partner who likes to scream and throw a tantrum when upset or a partner who easily breaks down and starts to cry when upset?

Would you rather be with someone who snores really loudly when asleep or someone who sleeps like a dead person?

Would you rather be with a computer geek or be with someone who has no idea on how to use technology?

Would you rather your partner was really hairy or didn't have a single hair on them?

Would you rather do romantic things or try out some new kinky ideas?

Would you rather End a first date with sex or with a passionate kiss?

Would you rather be caught cheating or catch your spouse cheating?

Would you rather let your significant other sleep with your best friend or sleep with your significant other's best friend?

Would you rather you bend down to kiss your significant other because of their height or stand on your tiptoe to kiss your significant other?

Would you rather your partner looked weak but was actually really strong or looked strong but was actually really weak?

Would you rather be with someone who always eats with their hands or someone who doesn't know how to use a fork and a knife?

Would you rather play your partner's favorite sport with them or cheer them as they play it with other people?

Would you rather your lover be one who likes to dress comfortably or one who likes to dress fashionably?

Would you rather have a partner who wears black all the time or who wears a lot of brightly colored clothes?

Would you rather have a partner who obsessed with hugs or who's obsessed with cuddles?

Would you rather go shopping for your significant other alone or go shopping with their best friend?

Would you rather have a partner that always looks nice or a partner that always smells nice?

Would you rather your partner had really long hair or no hair at all?

Would you rather your partner be one who's very popular on social media or one who's very popular in real life?

Would you rather be with someone who's always really late or who's always really early?

Would you rather babysit in place of your partner or babysit with them?

Would you rather have a partner with an infectious smile or an infectious laugh?

Would you rather video call all day or text each other all night?

Would you rather have a partner who loves to spend a lot or a partner who loves to save?

Would you rather go skydiving with your lover or go mountain climbing?

Would you rather have a partner who's a foodie or a partner who hardly ever eats?

Would you rather have a partner who takes a lot of selfies or one who takes a lot of pictures of you?

Would you rather have a partner who's very funny or a partner who's very ambitious?

Would you rather earn more than your significant other or have them earn more than you?

Would you rather be with someone who's feared or someone who's loved by all?

Would you rather spend your birthday with just your partner or spend it with your partner and some close friends?

Would you rather have a really small wedding with them or a really big wedding?

Would you rather go jogging together or go to the gym together?

Would you rather write love letters for your significant other or write them a song?

Would you rather have a lover who's obsessed with pets or one who doesn't like pets?

Would you rather make a gift by hand for your partner's birthday or purchase it from a store?

Would you rather your significant other was an atheist or was a very religious person?

Would you rather go somewhere sunny for your vacation or go somewhere really cold?

Would you rather have a driver to take you both around or do the driving by yourself all the time?

Would you rather give your partner a foot massage or a back massage?

Would you rather cook something with a lot of salt for dinner night or cook something with a lot of pepper?

Would you rather build a snowman together or roll around in the snow together?

Would you rather have a picnic together early in the morning as the sun rises or late in the evening as the sun sets?

Would you rather get something expensive and precious for your significant other or something cheap but very thoughtful?

Would you rather hold hands in public or have your hands around each other's waists in public?

Would you rather spend the entire day together or have a sleepover at night together?

Would you rather be with someone who knows how to play the instrument or someone who knows how to sing?

Would you rather do karaoke with your partner or watch your partner do karaoke?

Would you rather be with someone with a lot of class or someone with a lot of affluence?

Would you rather spend Christmas together or spend new year together?

Would you rather FaceTime each other or Skype each other?

Would you rather your partner worked in the army or worked with the navy?

Would you rather have a partner who uses glasses or a partner who wears contacts?

Would you rather your partner was from your hometown or your partner was from another continent?

Would you rather do some cooking together or do some baking together?

Would you rather find roses all over the house on date night or find scented candles all over the house?

Would you rather report your partner's wrongdoings to their folks or to their best friend?

Would you rather cuddle up all evening indoors or go watch the sunset together outside?

Would you rather slow dance to a romantic song together or grind to a fast beat?

Would you rather ride bikes side by side on take long walks side by side?

Would you rather take the most random selfies with your partner or go to a photo booth?

Would you rather you both went on a date dressed corporately or dressed casually?

Would you rather go jet-skiing together or go surfing together?

Would you rather go to a musical concert together or go to a drama festival together?

Would you rather share a bottle of wine together or share the same glass of wine?

Would you rather eat something exquisite and different together or eat pizza together?

Would you rather buy them a gift for valentine's day or make them a gift for valentine's day?

Would you rather get a tan at the beach together or go to a tanning salon together?

Would you rather go partying together or throw a party at home together?

Would you rather go to an art exhibition together or do an art exhibition together?

Would you rather dip your toes in the sand at the beach or draw your initials in the sand?

Would you rather go for a swim together or relax in a hot tub together?

Would you rather see your partner in baggy sweatshirts or in a sexy shirt?

Would you rather travel for a living together or travel as a hobby together?

Would you rather your partner owned a jet or owned a yacht?

Would you rather your partner was a science brainiac or one with an artistic soul?

Would you rather your partner has an excellent sense of smell or an excellent sense of hearing?

Would you rather your partner drinks only alcoholic drinks or refuses to touch anything that isn't water?

Would you rather watch Netflix together or watch YouTube videos together?

Would you rather listen to jazz music together or listen to blues together?

Would you rather rub your partner's back when they're sick or rub your partner's stomach when they're sick?

Would you rather be with someone who works from home or someone who goes to the office every morning?

Would you rather go to a formal event together or go to a casual event together?

Would you rather your partner was one that laughs a lot or one that makes you laugh a lot?

Would you rather be with a chef or be with a foodie?

Would you rather have your honeymoon somewhere popular and fancy or somewhere unknown and very homely?

Would you rather your partner had blue eyes or brown eyes?

Would you rather wear matching leather boots or matching sneakers?

Would you rather Choose a relationship with someone who is 10 years younger than you or someone who is 10 years older?

Would you rather be ghosted or get dumped over a phone call or over a text?

Would you rather marry someone you don't find physically attractive but has a great personality or someone who is great looking but doesn't have a personality you like?

Would you rather live without your boyfriend/girlfriend or without your best friend?

Would you rather spend your life with someone you don't love or with someone who doesn't love you back?

Would you rather be with someone who loves you more or with someone you love more?

Would you rather date someone you know nothing about or someone from your group of friends?

Would you rather would you rather have a fairytale wedding or a fairytale honeymoon?

Would you rather have a jealous partner or someone who doesn't care if you see other people?

Would you rather go for a one-night-stand or be in a 'friends with benefits' kind of relationship?

Would you rather have a bad relationship with your in-laws or for your spouse to have a bad relationship with your family and friends?

Would you rather move in with your partner before or after marriage?

Would you rather meet your soulmate and end up without them or never meet them?

Would you rather love someone unconditionally and have your heart broken forever or never have anyone love you?

Would you rather be with someone who thinks you are too clingy or have a too clingy partner?

Would you rather spend your life with a person more or less educated than you?

Would you rather be with someone more or less attractive than you?

Would you rather for your partner to have an emotional affair or to physically cheat on you?

Would you rather kiss your partner or hug them right now?

Would you rather text your partner you love them or say it to them in person?

Would you rather send your partner a good morning or a good night text?

Would you rather celebrate Valentine's day or your anniversary with your better half?

Would you rather have a romantic dinner or breakfast in bed?

Would you rather break someone's heart or let someone break your heart?

Would you rather have a partner who emotionally neglects you or a partner who is too clingy?

Would you rather tell someone you love them or have them tell you they love you?

Would you rather be a good kisser or great in bed?

Would you rather meet someone and fall in love with them over time or experience love at first sight?

Would you rather be unattractive and have an attractive partner or be attractive but have an unattractive partner?

Would you rather give up kissing or give up sex?

Would you rather keep a secret from your partner that is eating you alive or tell them that secret and hurt their feelings?

Would you rather drunkenly text your ex, telling them you still love them or get stopped by the police for drinking and driving?

Would you rather would you rather go back to the ex who has hurt you the most or end up alone?

Would you rather fall asleep next to the ex you hate or next to a complete stranger?

Would you rather know that you'll never find everlasting love or know that you'll always get cheated on?

Would you rather be with someone, knowing they don't love you or be with someone who cheated on you, knowing that they love you?

Would you rather live in a lie thinking that the person you love loves you back or know they don't have feelings for you?

Would you rather have an average love story that ends well or a once in a lifetime love story which ends up sadly?

Would you rather be in a relationship with someone who gets along with your best friend or with someone who gets along with your parents?

Would you rather confess your feelings to your crush or patiently wait for them to make the first move?

Would you rather get married in Las Vegas or have a traditional wedding?

Would you rather have your other half cook you a meal or take you out to a fancy dinner?

Would you rather go on vacation with your partner or with your friends?

Would you rather be with someone who hates your parents or with someone your parents hate?

Would you rather discover that your partner doesn't find you sexually attractive or that they are with you just to get into your pants?

Would you rather be extremely jealous but never get cheated on or to have your partner constantly cheat on you without you ever suspecting a thing?

Would you rather have your partner cheat on you with a different person every month for a year or cheat on you with one person for twelve months?

Would you rather have a person by your side who has completely different worldviews than you or someone who has completely different interests than you?

Would you rather be with someone who is terrible in bed but can make you laugh or with someone who is incredibly boring but great in bed?

Would you rather lose all of your photos ever taken with your partner or lose everything they've ever given you?

Would you rather marry someone you love who is poor or someone you don't love who is incredibly wealthy?

Would you rather live for 100 years without ever having love or live for 30 years with your true soulmate?

Would you rather be with someone who is a good person but whom you don't truly love or with someone who is a bad person but is your real love?

Would you rather be in a relationship while still having feelings for your ex or in a relationship where your partner still has feelings for their ex?

Would you rather spend your entire life with the person who gave you your first passionate kiss or with the person you lost your virginity with?

Would you rather be ghosted or told that you got dumped because you are unattractive?

Would you rather get a horrible present from your partner or give them something you see they don't like?

Would you rather break up with your partner on your anniversary or while you two are on a road trip?

Would you rather stay friends with your ex or never talk to them again?

Would you rather cheat on your partner or propose a threesome?

Would you rather know your partner cheated on you or never find out about it?

Would you rather be with someone who stops loving you after a while or with someone who never loved you back?

Would you rather hang out with your partner's ex or have your partner hang out with your ex?

Would you rather have children with someone you don't love or be with someone you love but without ever being able to have children?

Would you rather do it in missionary with someone who turns you on or have wild sex with someone you don't find attractive?

Would you rather do it on the kitchen table or on the kitchen floor?

Would you rather have sex in the car or in a house filled with other people?

Would you rather get caught doing it by your parents or catch your parents doing it?

Would you rather try a threesome with your ex or with your partner's ex?

Would you rather read an erotic novel or watch porn?

Would you rather sext or talk dirty over the phone?

Would you rather have phone or cam sex?

Would you rather be submissive or dominant in the bedroom?

Would you rather make love or have a quickie?

Would you rather do it doggy or girl on top style?

Would you rather have sex in the shower or in the bathtub?

Would you rather talk dirty during sex or be completely silent while doing it?

Would you rather have your partner watch you sleep with someone else or watch them do it with someone else?

Would you rather have sex ten times a day or not have it for an entire year?

Would you rather give up sex for good or have bad sex from now on?

Would you rather have a threesome with someone you know or invite a complete stranger in your bedroom?

Would you rather would you rather have sex in the club bathroom or in the airplane bathroom?

Would you rather do it on a live webcam or make a sex tape?

Would you rather be an escort or a porn star?

Would you send your nudes to a stranger or send your nudes to an ex?

Would you rather sleep with someone twice your age or a minor?

Would you rather touch yourself in private or in the presence of your significant other?

Would you rather give a lap dance or a strip tease?

Would you rather be horny all the time or never be able to have an orgasm?

Would you rather have a one night stand with someone really attractive or someone really skilled in bed?

Would you rather know that you can't please your partner in bed or spend your life in ignorance, thinking you are giving them pleasure?

Would you rather pay for sex or get paid for sex?

Would you rather be with someone who stares at you a lot or one who loves to have your attention all the time?

Would you rather read a book together or listen to an audiobook together?

Would you rather buy a penthouse together or buy a beach house together?

Would you rather live in a town together or live in a city together?

Would you rather have the lights on or off during foreplay?

Would you rather have group sex with strangers or with all your exes?

Would you rather only have sex in the bedroom or never have sex in the bedroom?

Would you rather have sex in the backyard or on the front porch?

Would you rather have early morning sex or late night sex?

Would you rather make out with your boss or watch your partner make out with their boss?

Would you rather have kinky sex or romantic sex?

Would you rather finger/be fingered under the table of a busy restaurant or under the table at your parent's place?

Would you rather have sex with a corpse or never have sex again?

Would you rather know when your parents are having sex or have your parents know when you're having sex?

Would you rather sleep with a superior at work for a raise or find out your partner sleep with a superior at work for a raise?

Would you rather make out in the dark or make out in public?

Would you rather have sex up against the wall or in bed?

Would you rather take off your partner's underwear with your teeth or tease them with your tongue till they take off their underwear?

Would you rather make a lot of noises during sex or a really loud noise during orgasm?

Would you rather be with someone who loves to strip tease or who knows how to tease with their lips

Would you rather suck at foreplay or suck at sex?

Would you rather be with someone who walks around the house naked all the time or someone who wears the most seductive outfits around the house?

Would you rather watch your dog have sex with another dog or watch strangers have sex?

Would you rather make out on a bed filled with stains or on a dusty bedroom floor?

Would you rather be horny a lot or hardly ever get horny?

Would you rather your most hated ex, threaten to upload a sex video of you and your current lover or a sex video of you masturbating?

Would you rather have sex in the boardroom at your office or in the parking lot?

Would you rather have rough sex or gentle sex?

Would you rather accidentally send a dirty text message to your boss or your partner's mom?

Would you rather make out with someone else or watch your partner make out with someone else?

Would you rather make love beside a fireplace or in the rain?

Would you rather be pregnant or have an incurable STI after a one night stand

Would you rather have sex on a busy bus or in a busy bus's dirty bathroom?

Would you rather eavesdrop on another couple having sex or be eavesdropped on during sex?

Would you rather your significant other striptease in public for strangers or striptease in private for friends?

Would you rather tie your partner in bed or have your partner tie you up in bed?

Would you rather have your partner rub your genitals while driving to work or rub your genitals while you're at work?

Would you rather have foreplay without penetration or penetration without any foreplay?

Would you rather have sex inside a car or on the bonnet of a car?

Would you rather have a threesome without your significant other's knowledge or watch your significant other participate in a threesome without you?

Would you rather be blindfolded during sex or blindfold your partner during sex?

Would you rather your significant other used ice cubes to tease you during foreplay or used candle wax to tease you during foreplay?

Would you rather have drunk sex or stoned sex?

Would you rather act porn with your partner but be unpopular or act porn with a stranger and be very popular?

Would you rather get instantly horny every time you saw your significant other or instantly have an orgasm every time you saw your significant other?

Would you rather have more foreplay with your partner or more sex with your partner?

Would you rather your lover had a one night stand with their high school crush or with a total stranger?

Would you rather find out your lover had sex with their ex or your lover had sex with their distant cousin?

Would you rather have rough sex all the time or have gentle sex all the time?

Would you rather make out with your lover in front of their parents or in front of their siblings?

Would you rather have a lover who loves to give you kinky nicknames in bed or a lover who loves to scream your real name in bed?

Would you rather have a sex video of you and your lover get to your extended family or get to your younger siblings?

Would you rather have sex with someone who never showers or someone who never brushes their teeth?

Would you rather read 50 Shades Of Grey or watch 50 Shades Of Grey?

Would you rather have sex in extreme cold or in extreme warmth?

Would you rather make out in a hallway or make out in a storage room?

Would you rather your partner talked dirty to you in a sexy French accent or in a sexy British accent?

Would you rather make love under the stars or under the rain?

Would you rather have sex doggy style all your life or missionary style all your life?

Would you rather find a text of your significant other sending nudes or asking for nudes?

Would you have sex with just your entire family watching or with your entire neighborhood watching?

Would you rather make love to your partner with the lights on and the curtains wide open or with the lights off and the curtains closed?

Would you rather shower with your lover's best friend or let your lover shower with your best friend?

Would you rather get a sexy massage with maple syrup or a sexy massage with hot sauce?

Printed in Great Britain
by Amazon